BELOGNS TO:

_____

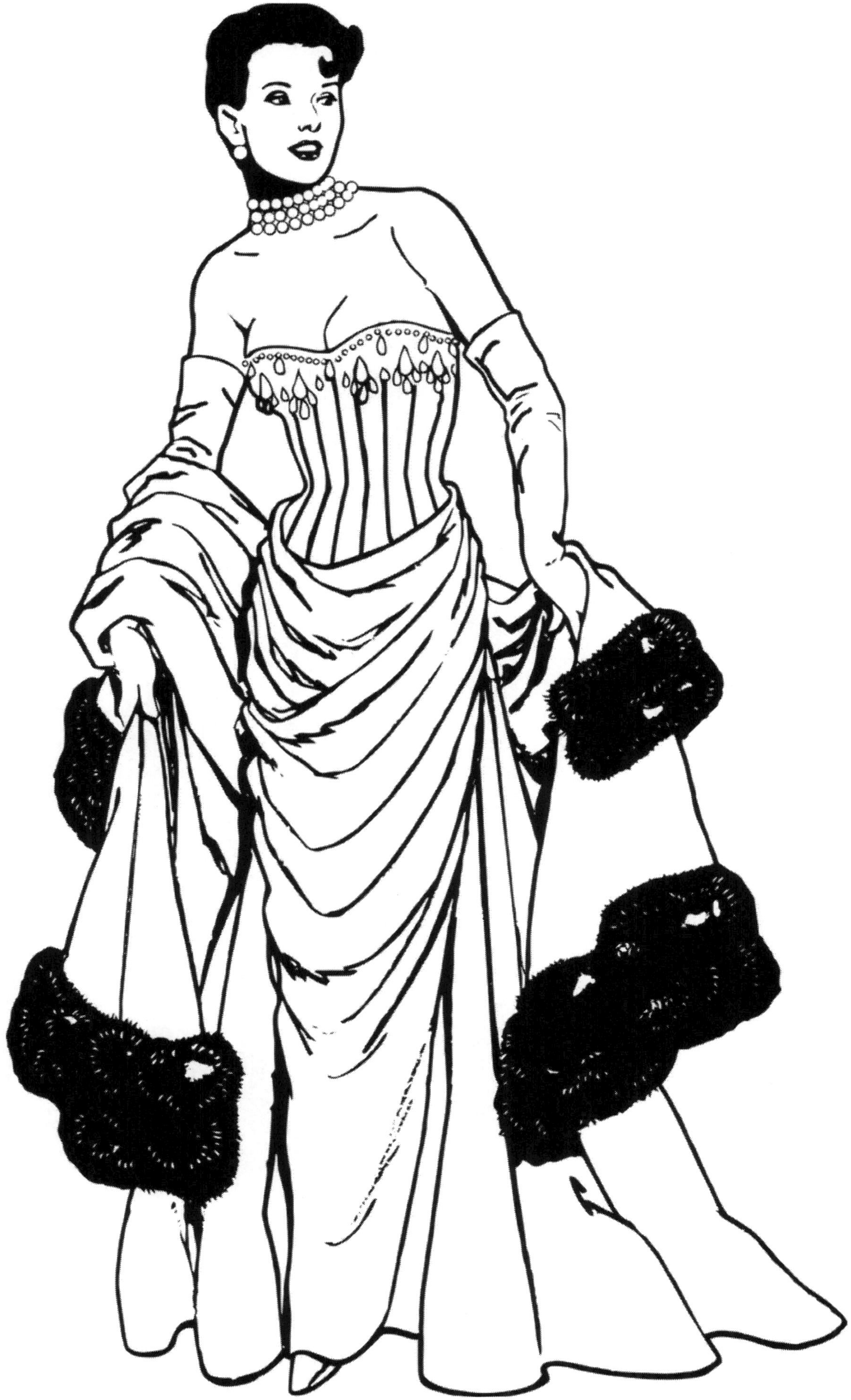

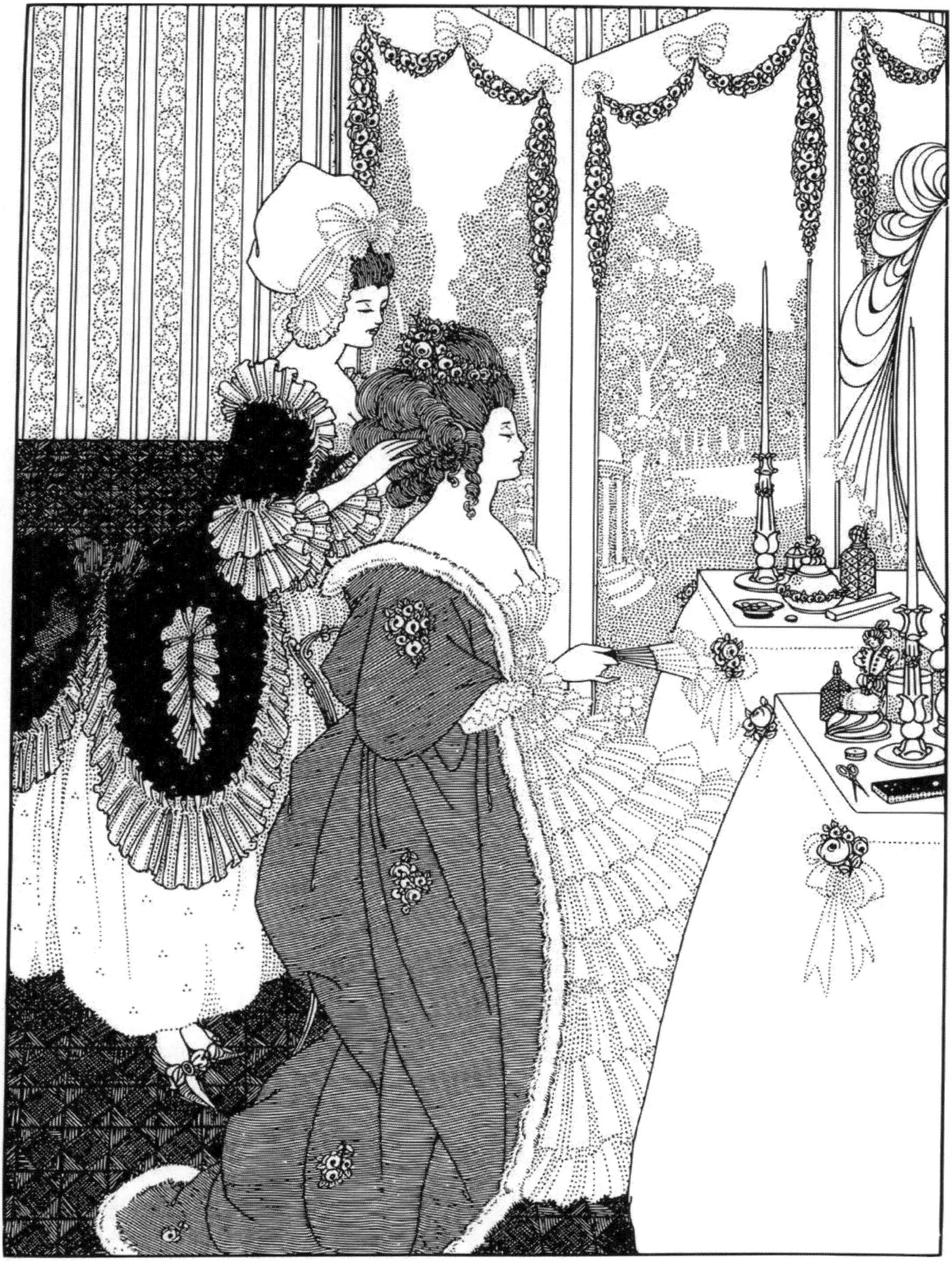

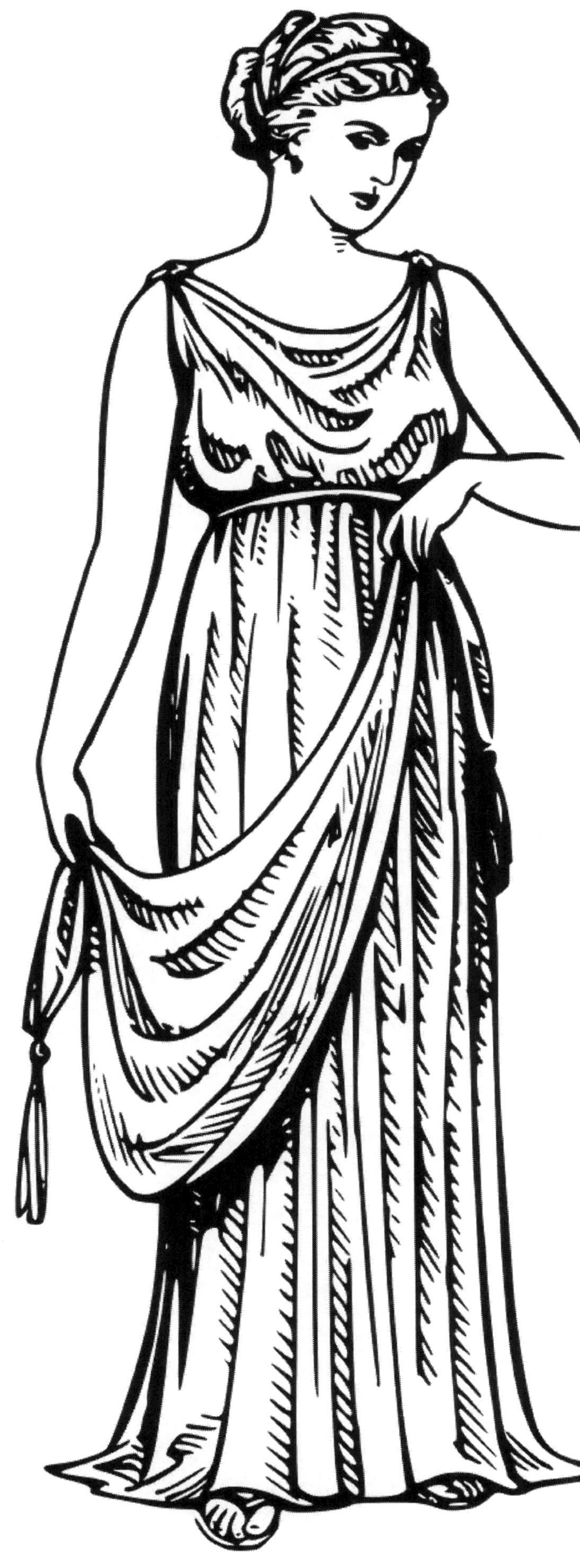

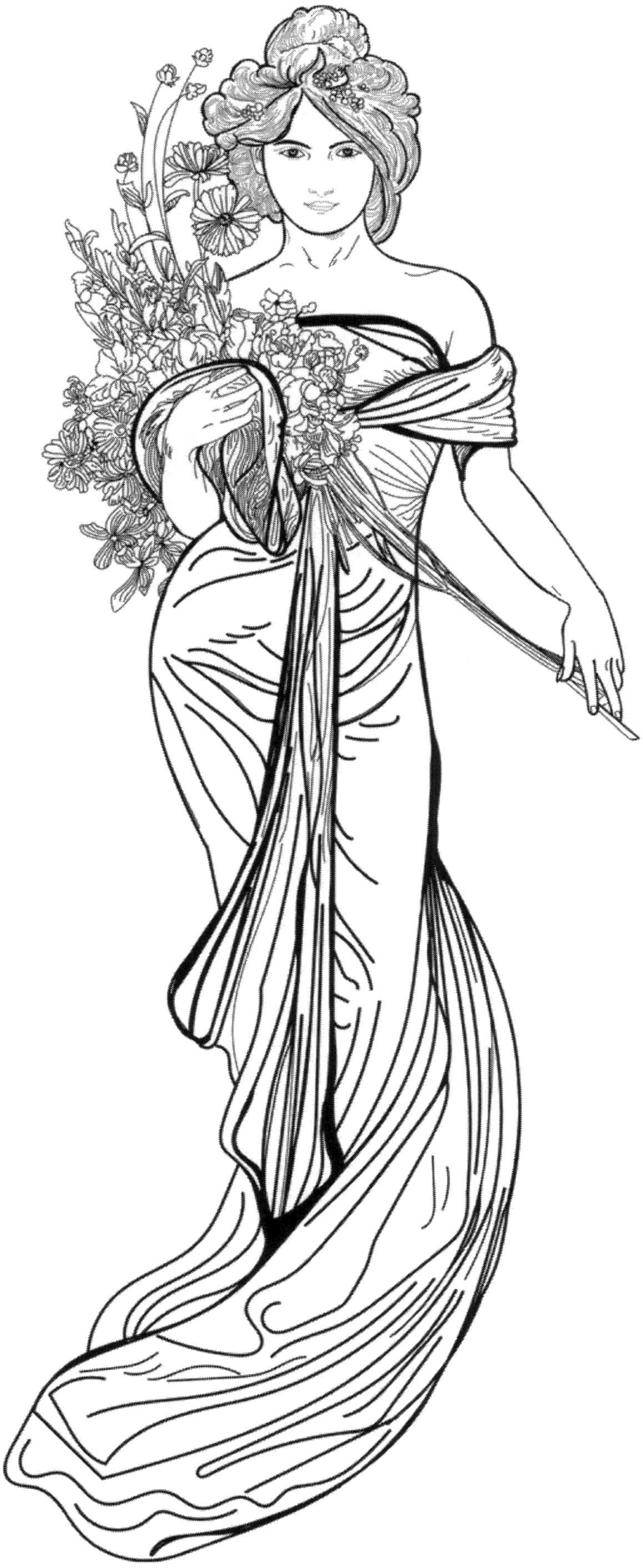

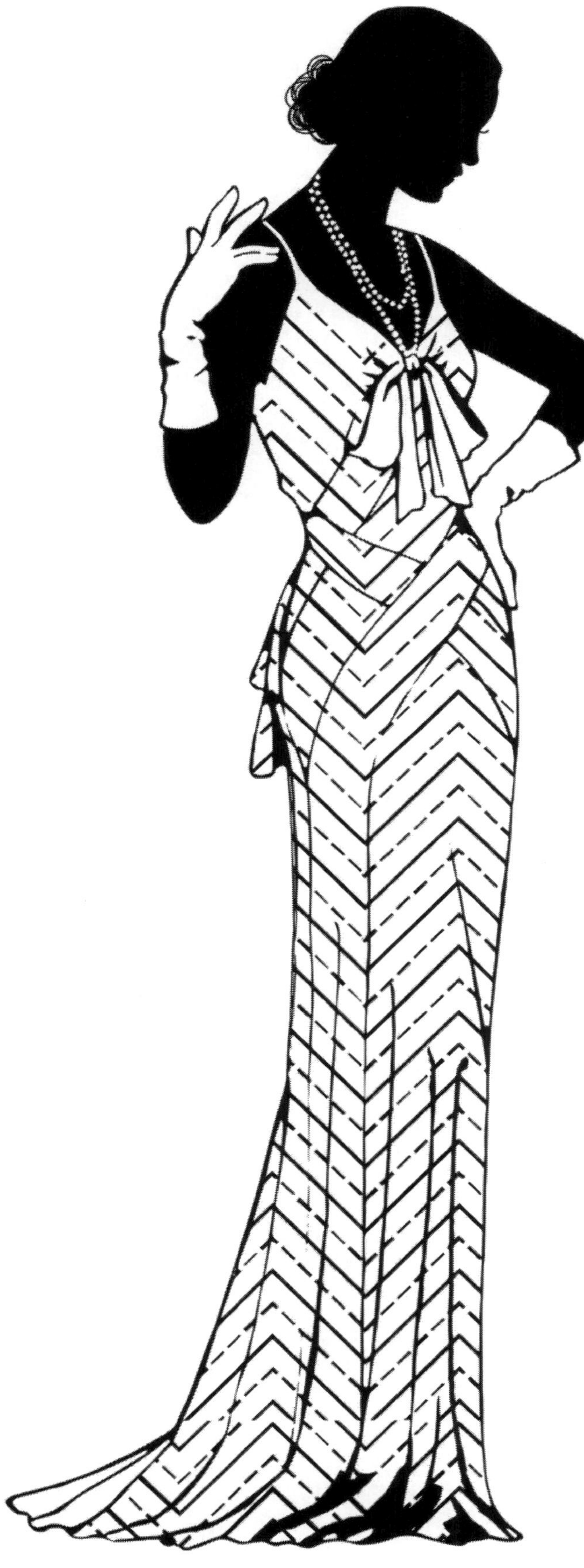

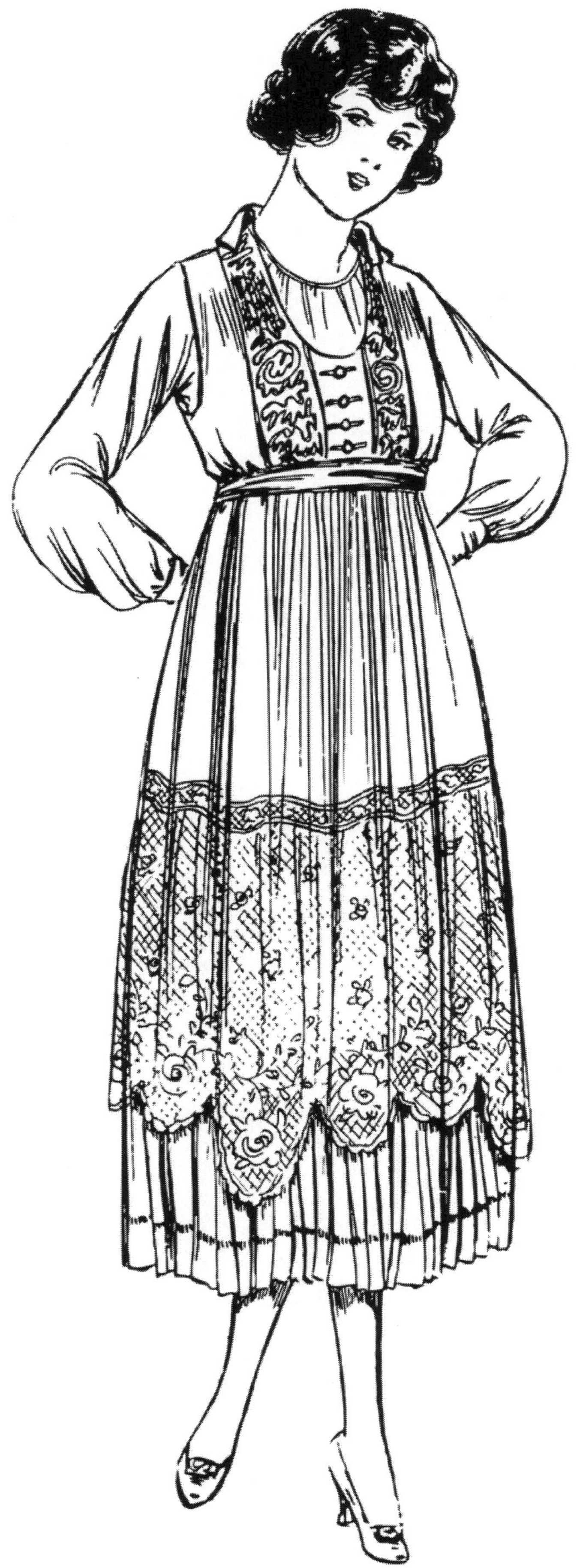

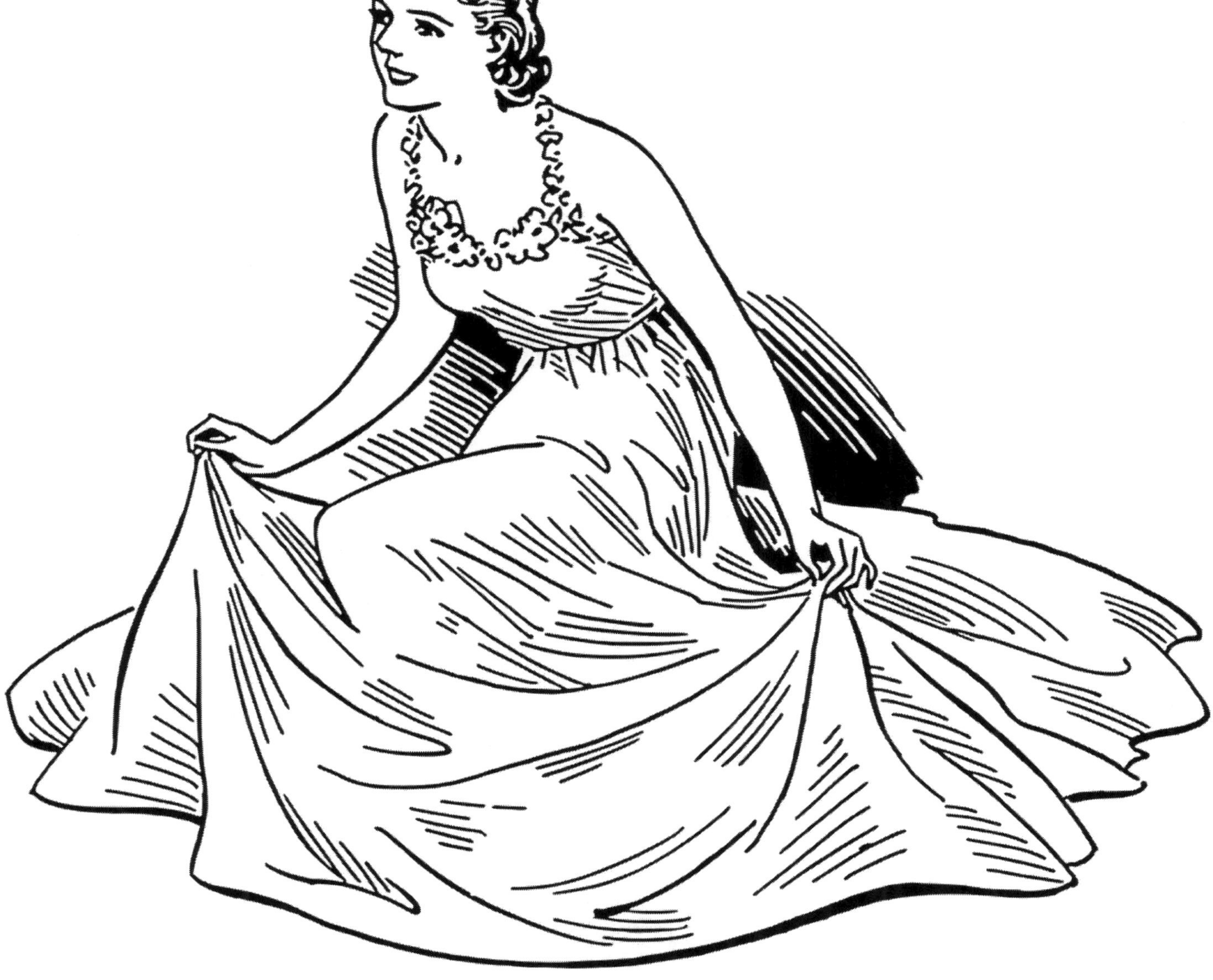

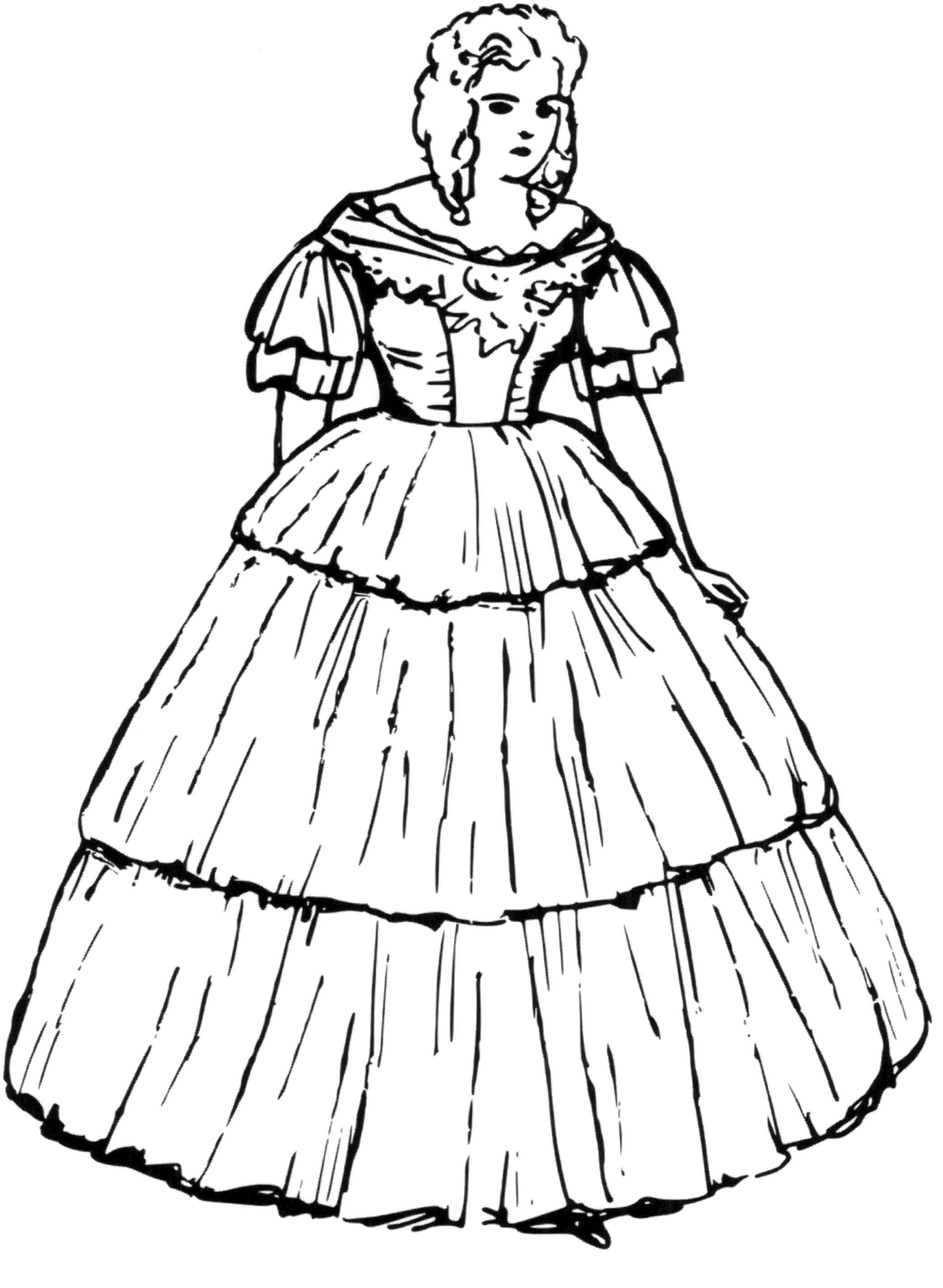

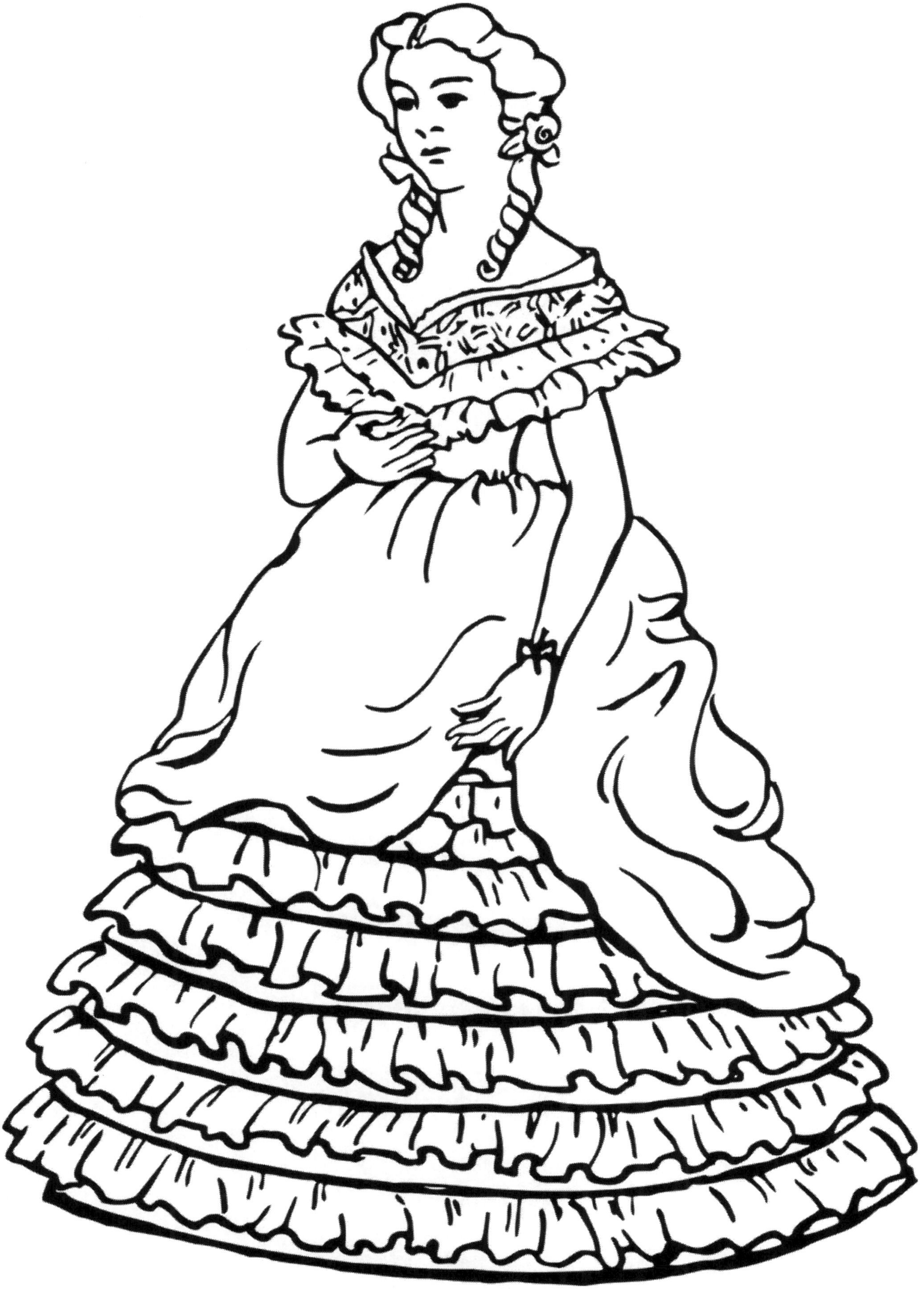

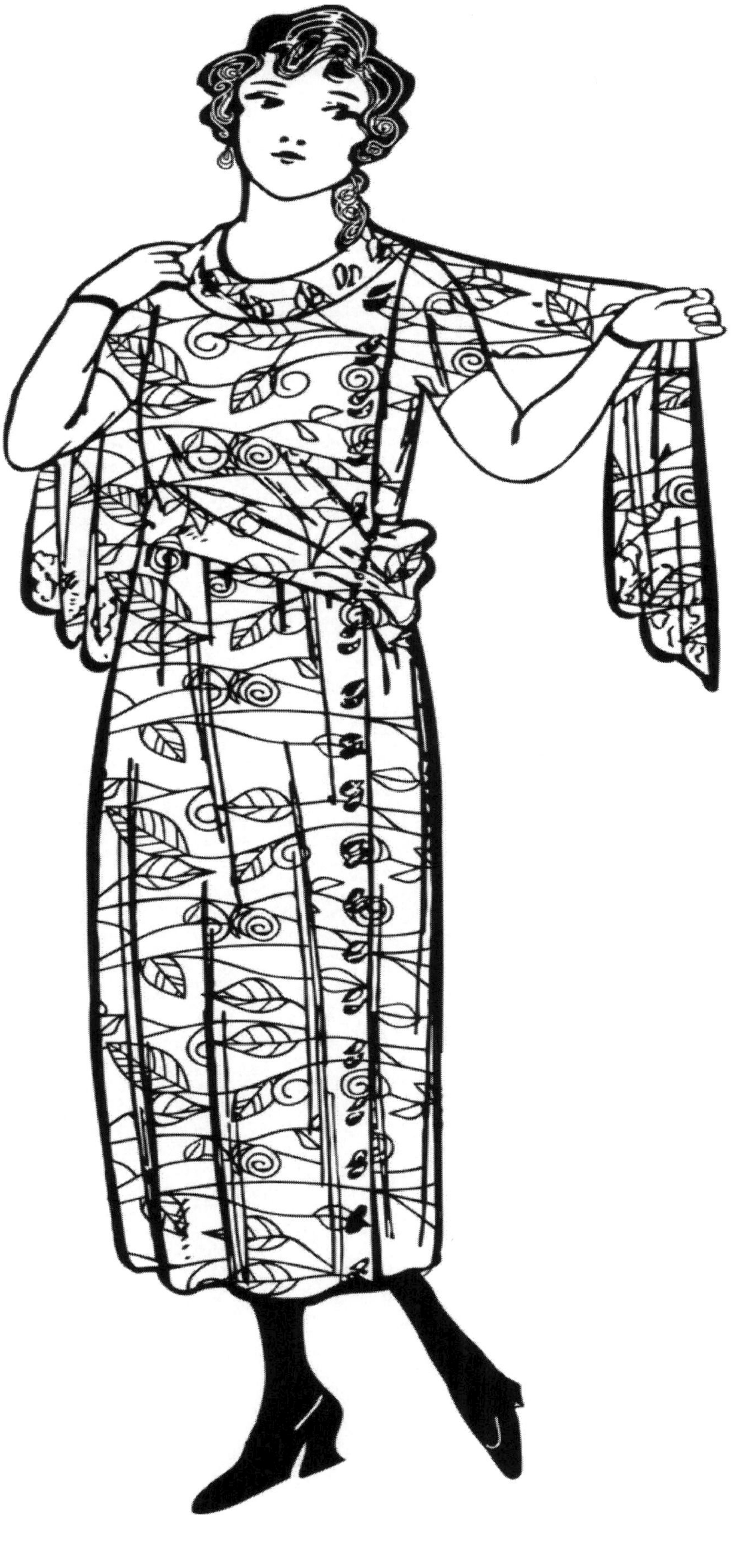

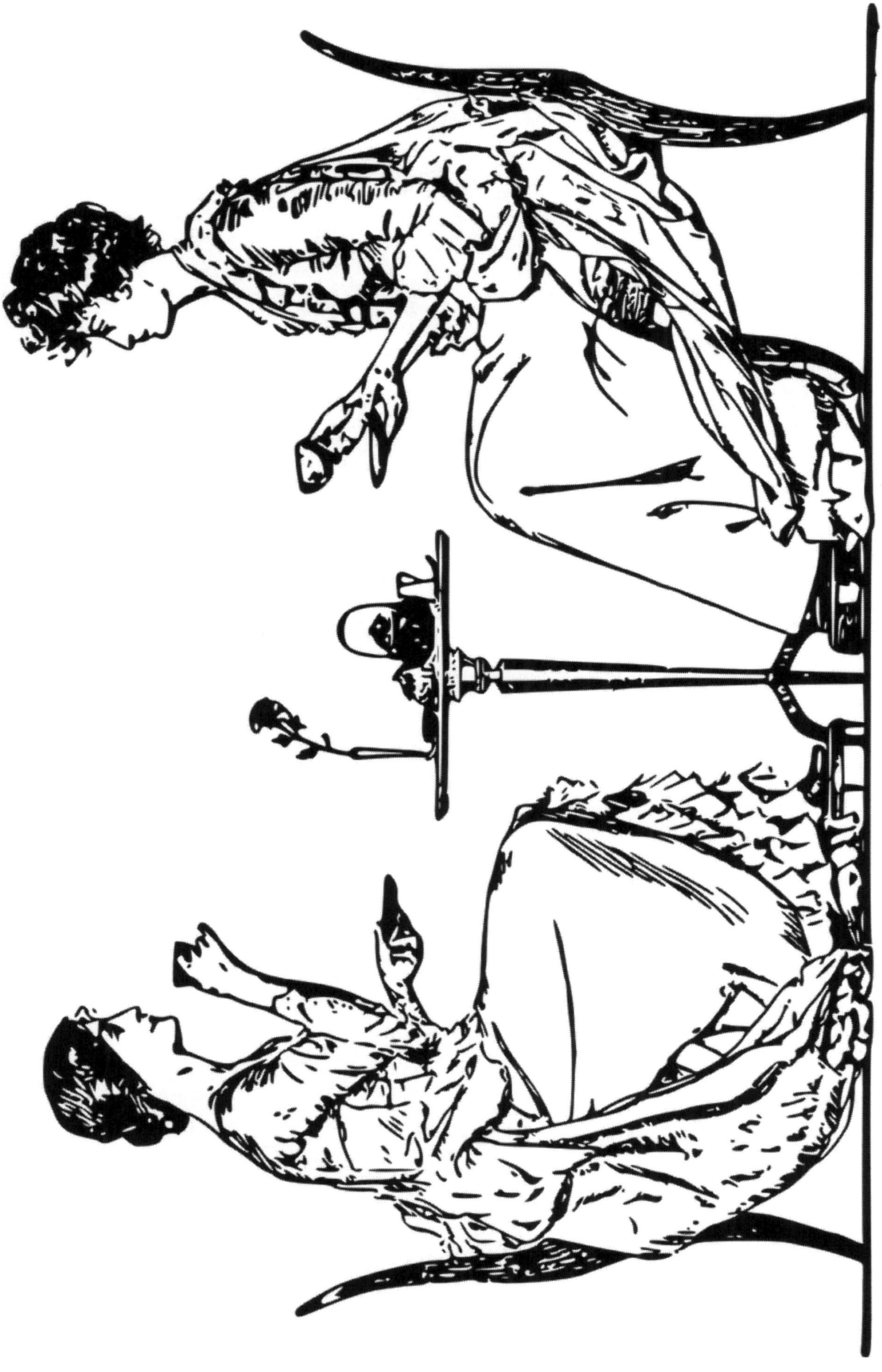

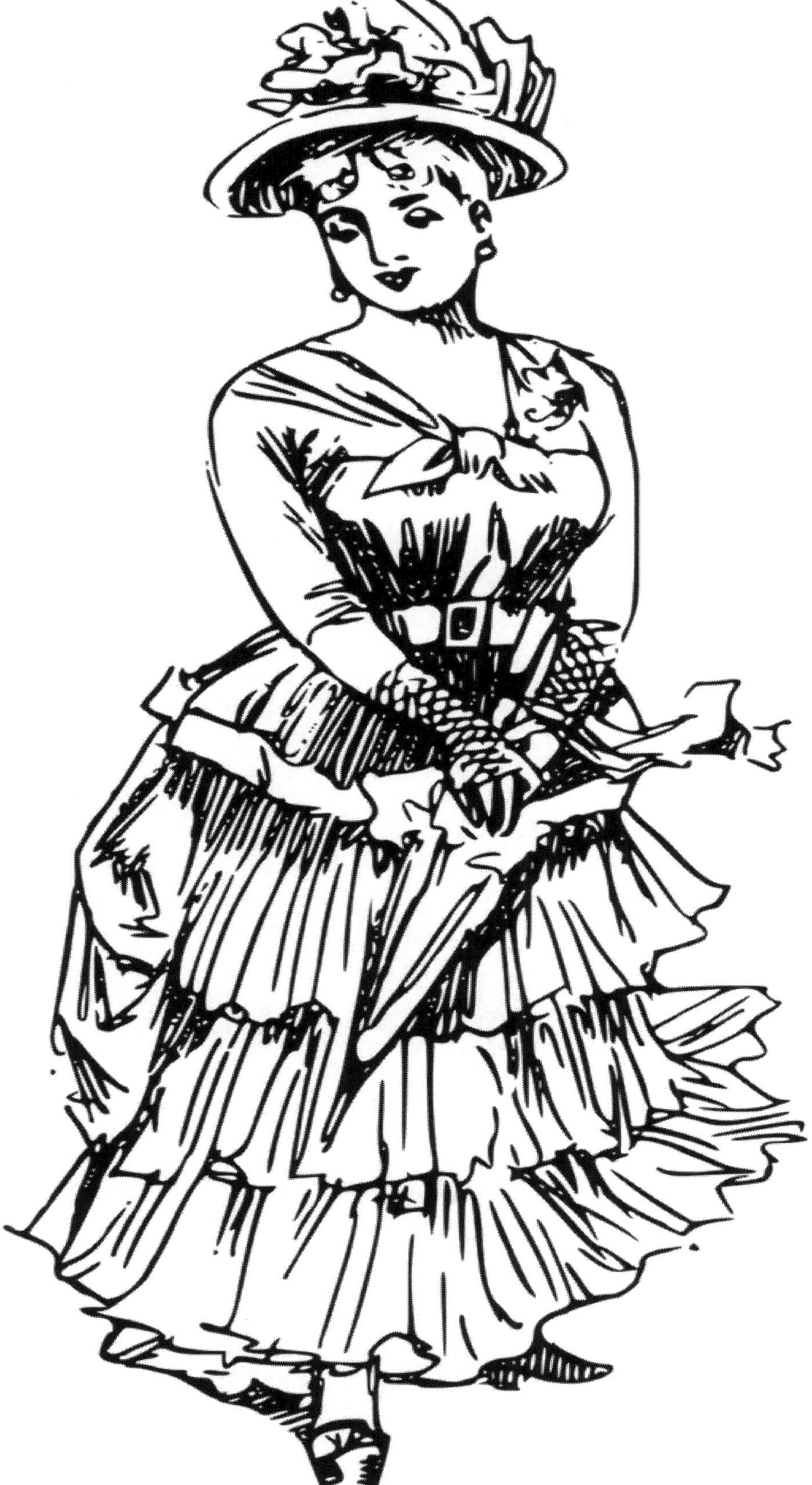

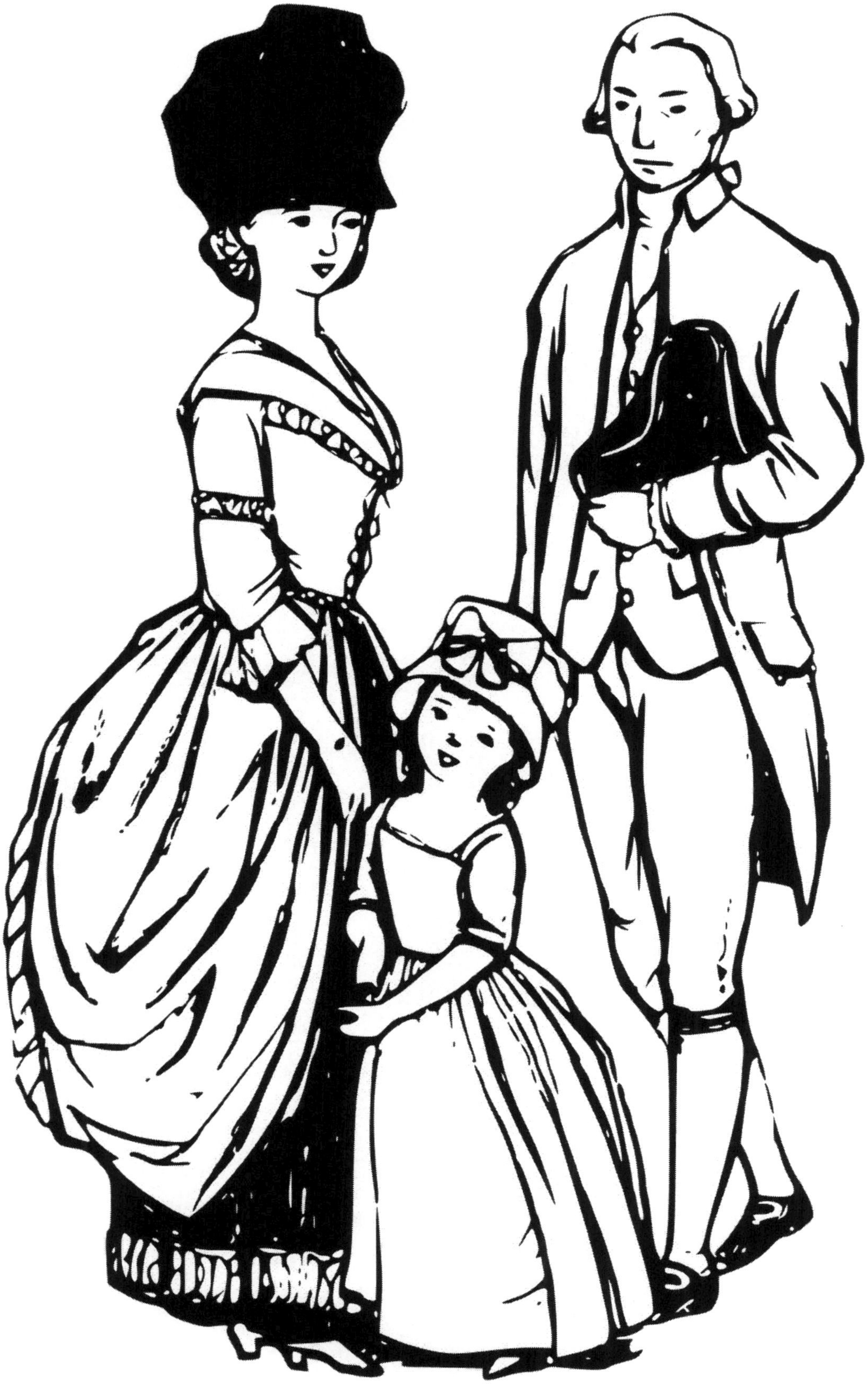

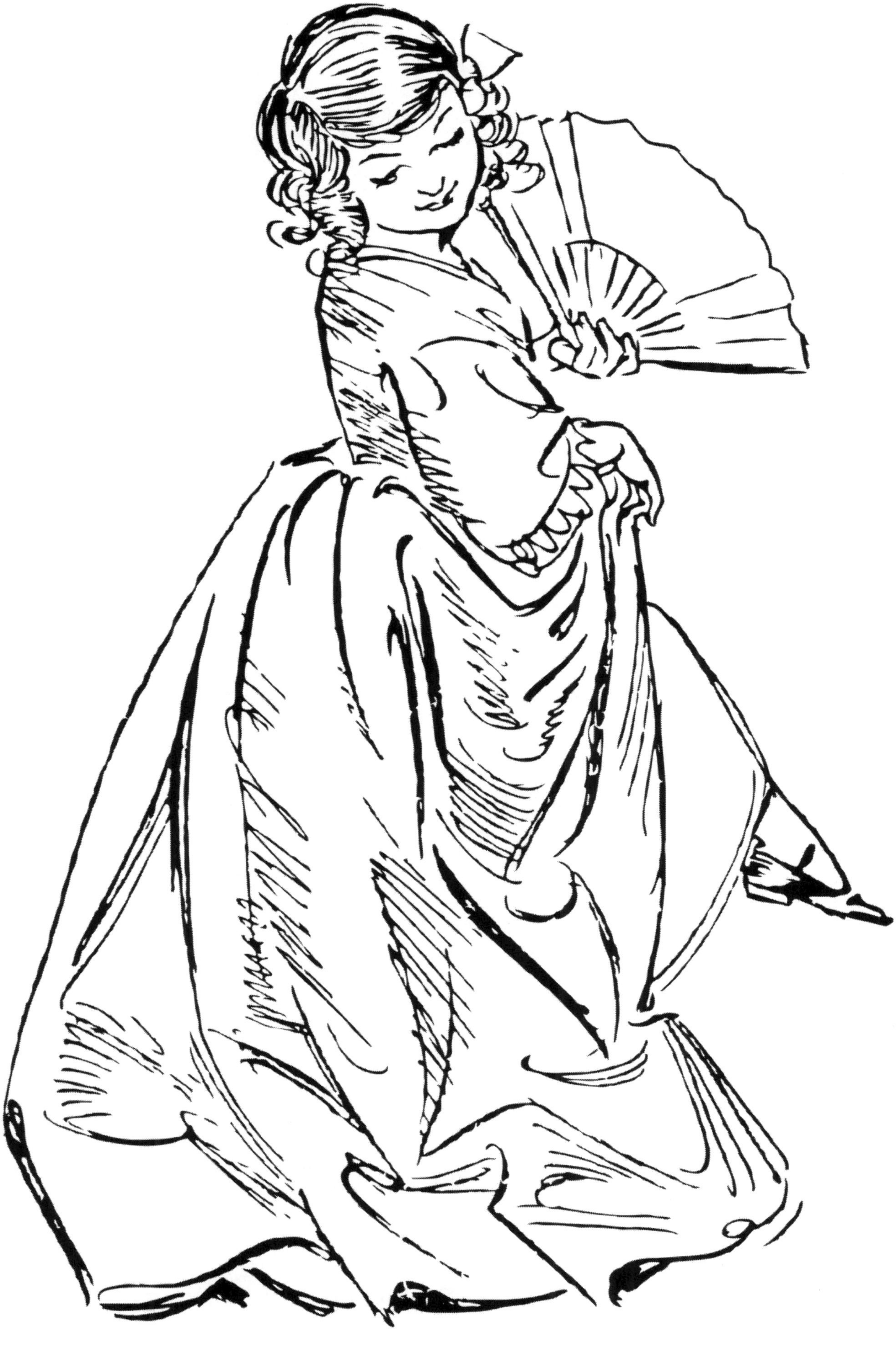

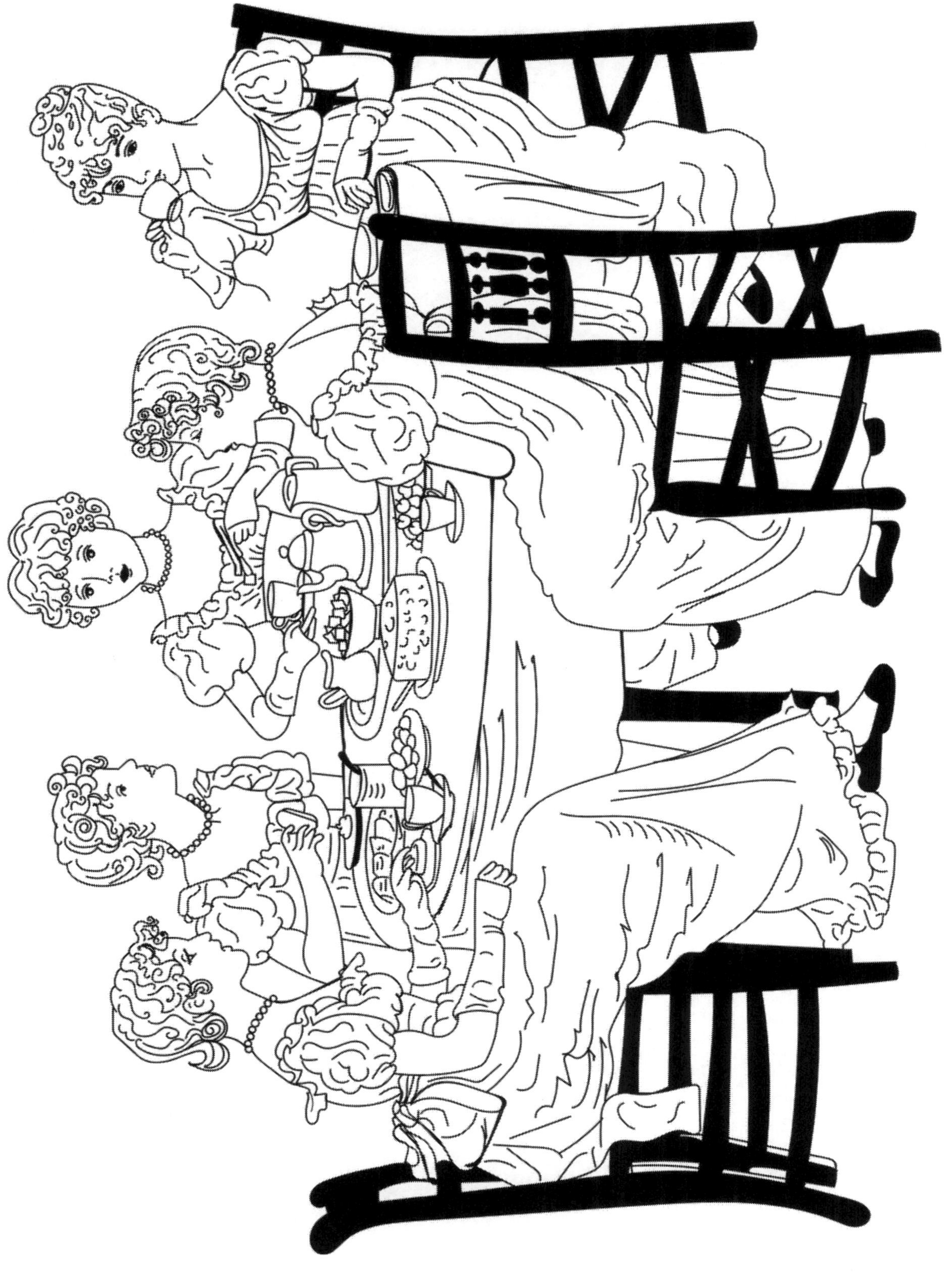

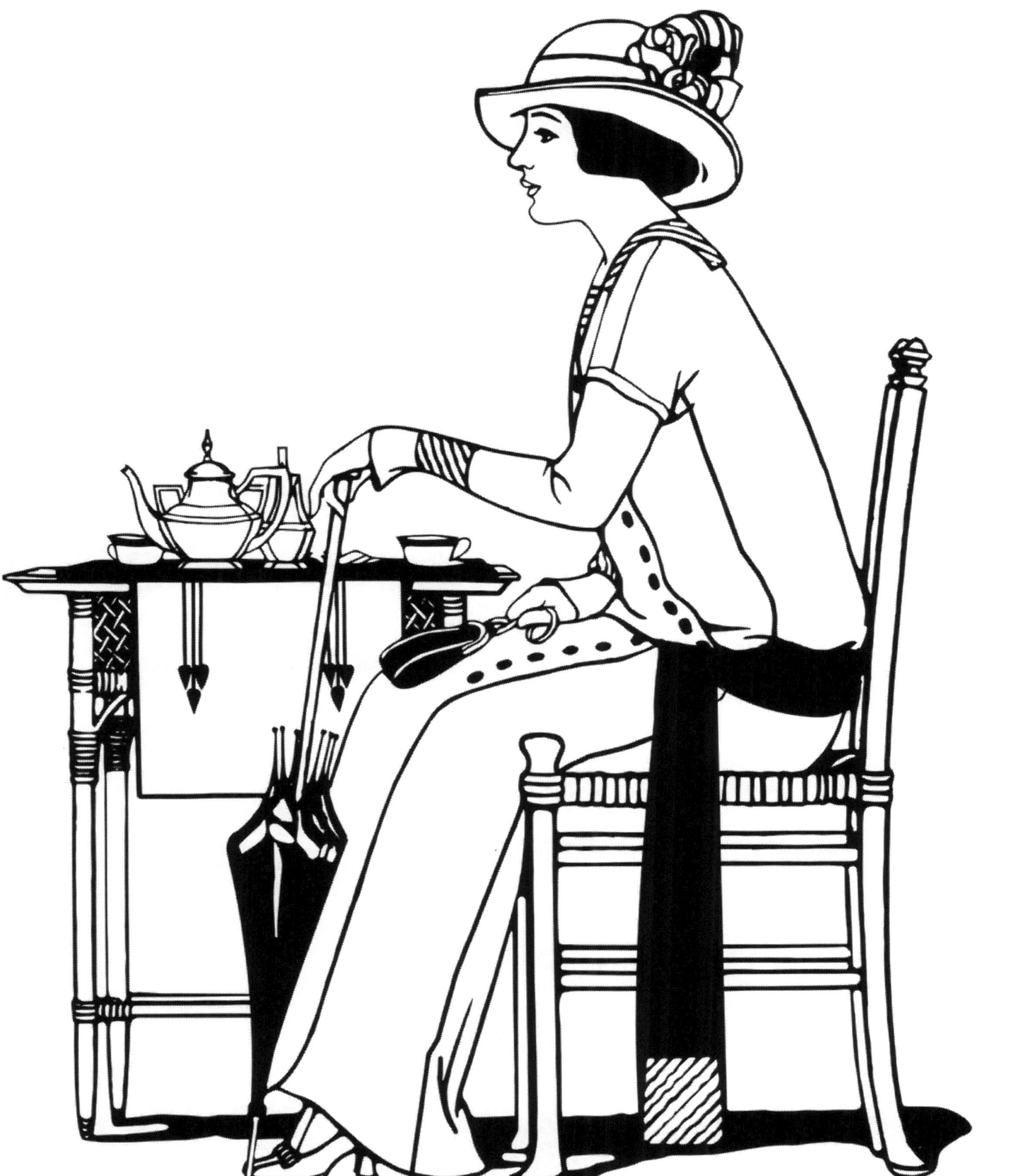

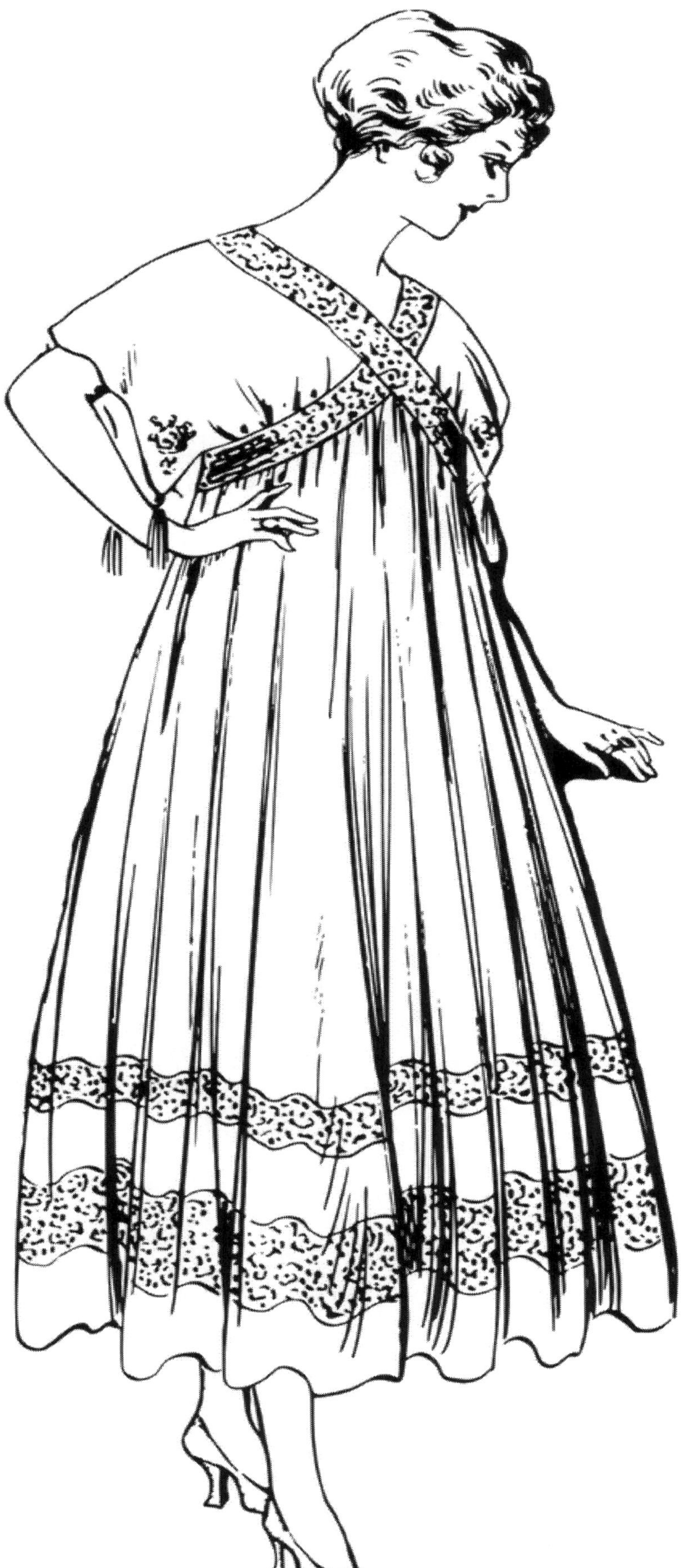

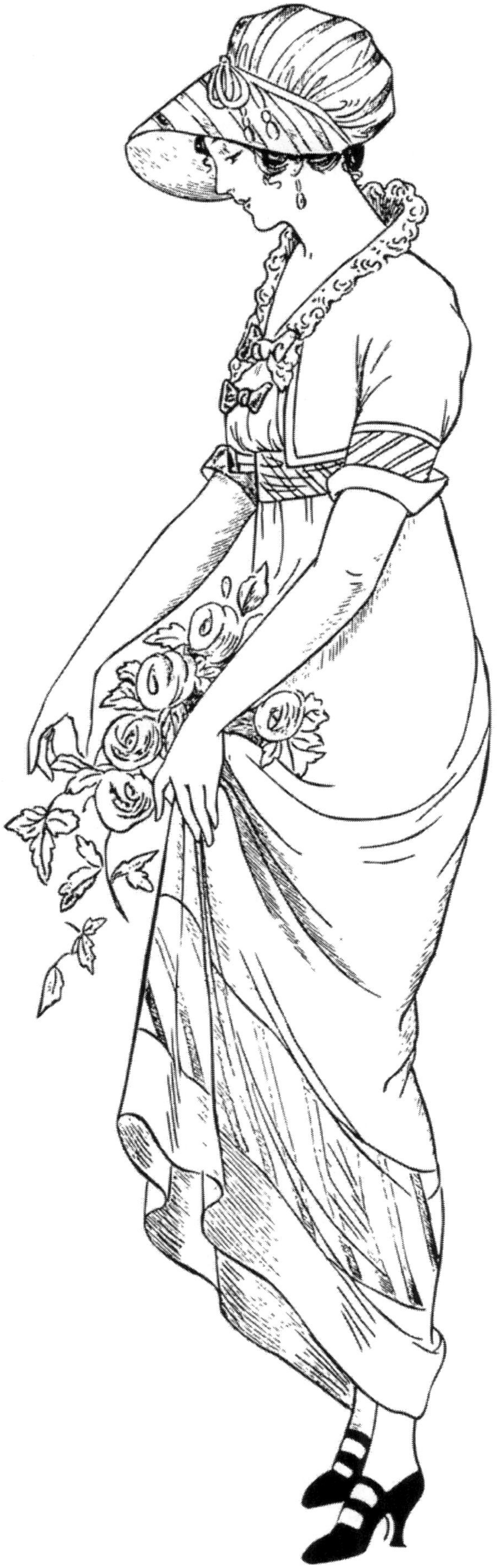

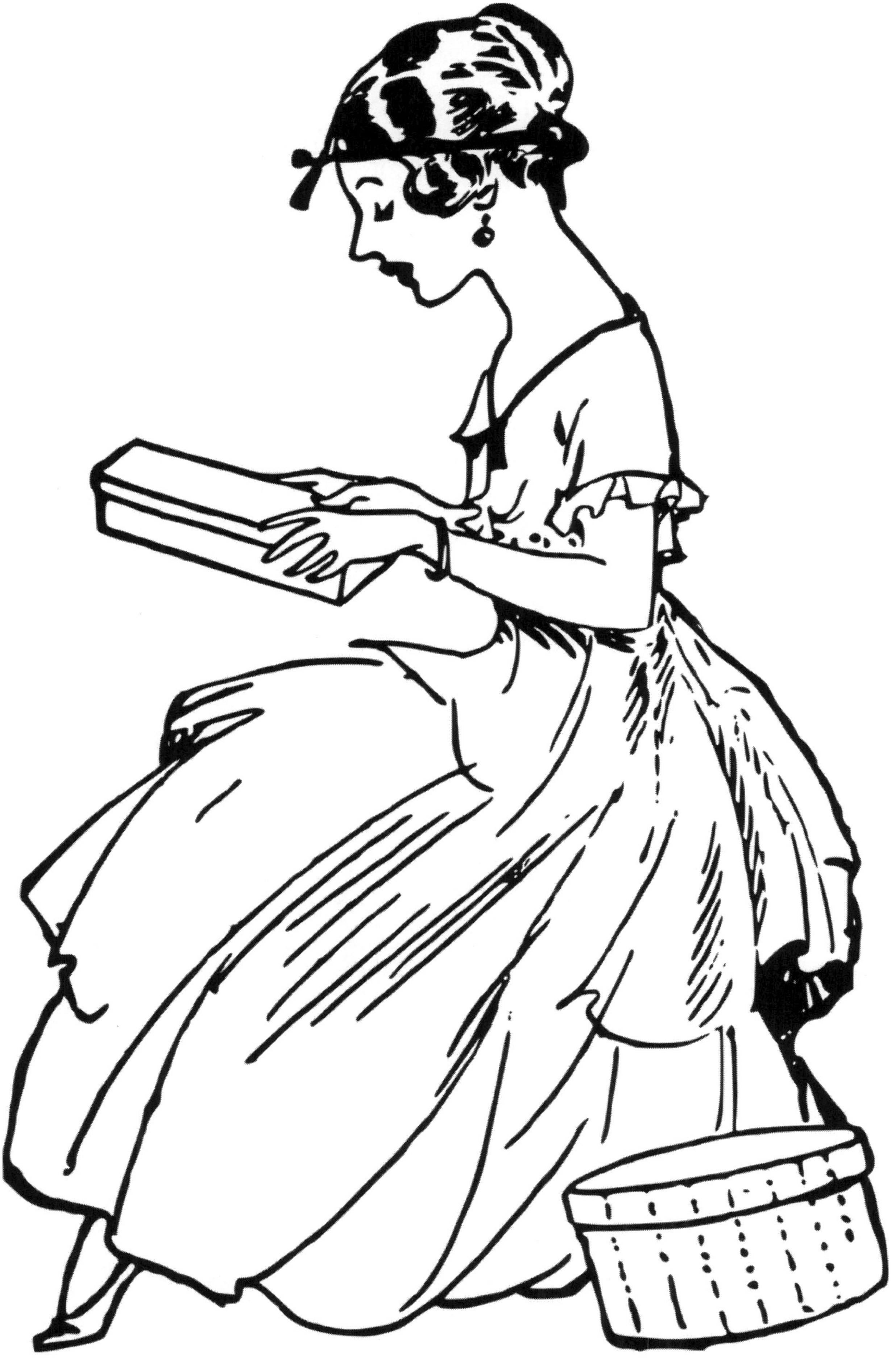

We hope to meet your expectations Share your opinion in the comments, it will be very motivating for us to continue and make our book appear to many people

Made in the USA
Middletown, DE
10 May 2021